INDIAN ROCK CARVINGS

INDIAN ROCK CARVINGS
OF THE PACIFIC NORTHWEST

BY EDWARD MEADE

go

Gray's Publishing Ltd.
Sidney, British Columbia, Canada.

Book design E. W. Harrison
Printed and bound in Canada by
Evergreen Press Limited
Vancouver, British Columbia

SBN 0-88826-027-X

For Michael
who shared many trips.

Foreword

One of the kinds of archaeological research which is often done better by "amateurs" than by their professional colleagues is the seeking out and recording of the prehistoric carvings on rock faces known as petroglyphs, and their painted counterparts, pictographs. The task is one best done by a dedicated and patient sleuth who knows and loves the outdoors and is willing to devote a great deal of time and effort to the search. The few professional archaeologists who have worked along the Northwest Coast have usually recorded whatever petroglyphs they encountered during their general surveys of archaeological sites, but they have seldom been able to take the time to do a thorough job. More of a contribution in this field has been made by a small number of distinguished amateurs, who have pursued the search as a hobby, putting into it more passion than most men put into their professions. Ed Meade is such a man, and this book is his compilation, many years in the making, of almost all known petroglyphs along the coast between Alaska and the Columbia River.

There can be a great fascination in finding and contemplating these strange representations left by the Indian people of hundreds or thousands of years ago. Petroglyphs tend to be stubbornly inscrutable things, since the ways of determining their age and meaning are so few. Depending on your temperament and your training, this can add either to the frustration or the fascination. With a little imagination, standing on the same lonely beaches where the ancient artists once stood, you can feel a kind of kinship with them. You cannot help but speculate on what they were trying to portray. The very mystery unfetters the imagination, and you think of solitary shamans imbued with visions of their spirit helpers and trying to record them at remote places of supernatural power, of secret societies, of cannibal spirits, perhaps even of sacrifices. Such speculations are not without support in the evidence that does exist, and they can be indulged more freely by laymen than by professional archaeologists bound by the constraints of scientific caution. There is a place for scientific caution, but there is also a place for insightful speculation.

The interpretation of petroglyphs is not wholly a matter of speculation. The book contains some acute observations on the styles of these strangely varying rock carvings, and on their locations. Ed Meade has some very interesting things to say about the ones which are now found below the high tide line, and were likely made at a time in the remote past when the ocean level was lower than at present. Again, the degree of erosion of a petroglyph can depend on its openness to exposure, but it can also be a measure of its age. When the same site has petroglyphs of great differences in age, we must wonder what it was that caused people to return to it century after century to leave their marks. With such observations, combined with observations of changes in "style"—that elusive combination of attributes that reveals itself to the practiced eye—we begin to perceive patterns which can be read as history.

To take a good photograph of an old and eroded petroglyph, as many of us have learned to our dismay, is no easy matter. With the right angle of light and the right combination of skill and luck, it is sometimes possible to bring out all the detail that is there. It often involves waiting patiently for shadows to move, or returning at a better time. One of the strengths of this book is the fine quality of most of the photographs, especially those taken by Ed Meade himself at the rich sites close to his home area of Vancouver Island. Earlier photographers sometimes yielded to the temptation to trace the carvings with chalk, a misguided (and now probably illegal) practice that defaces the petroglyphs and inevitably imposes some degree of reinterpretation of the designs. Fortunately, new methods are being developed to copy the designs by means of rubbings, which give clarity and fidelity of detail without defacing or otherwise harming the originals.

While there is much value in publishing books such as this on the monuments of the past, there is unfortunately some danger as well. The added publicity increases the traffic of visitors to the sites, which sometimes results in vandalism. Governments may pass laws to protect them (in British Columbia all petroglyphs and pictographs are protected by the provincial Archaeological and Historic Sites Protection Act), but that is not enough. They must also be protected by the respect in which people hold them. Readers of this book will certainly become conscious of the great affection which Ed Meade holds for these ancient records of the past. It is to be hoped that they will follow his example and respect them too.

Wilson Duff, Associate Professor, Dept. of Anthropology and Sociology, University of British Columbia.

Introduction

Primitive man throughout the world has left his record in rock paintings and carvings, in caves, on rock outcroppings, glacial erratics and beach boulders. Some of the paintings in France, Spain and Siberia depict animals that have long been extinct, and from this archaeologists have been able to date them to very early periods in man's history. On the other hand, the rock carvings of the world have so far offered no opportunity for dating, so that we do not know if they were done a few hundred years ago, or far back in time.

Nor do we know why early man carved the petroglyphs. We can only guess. The carvings throughout the world range widely in style and subject representations, and there would seem to be no relationship between areas. In North America, the distribution is relatively dense in some regions, nonexistent in others, and as in the rest of the world, styles and subject matter vary greatly between areas. The petroglyphs of the Northwest Coast are unique in that some of them bear a similarity to petroglyphs in Far Eastern Siberia and to some in the South Pacific.

The trail of the coast petroglyphs, if it can be called that, begins in Alaska and leads southward down the coast to Washington, where it turns into Puget Sound and the Columbia River. There it ends abruptly. Rock carvings of the interior high plateau, and to the south of the Columbia, in southwestern Oregon, are of a totally different genre.

But did the trail of the petroglyphs lead southward from Alaska, or northward out of the Columbia River? There is no answer. If they were carved by a people from the interior who migrated to the coast, we should expect to find evidence of their carving behind them in the continental interior. But this is not so.

If they were a coastal maritime people who vanished into the Columbia River country, we should still look for evidence of their carving in the interior. But the trail of the coast style of petroglyphs ends at the Dalles on the lower Columbia River.

Why the coast petroglyphs are distinct and different from the interior carvings may remain a mystery. One would expect them to merge with those of the interior plateau, or with those in central Oregon, that there would exist a transitional area in Washington or Oregon where the interior style would exhibit some of the coast attributes in a changing form. But the change between the styles is marked and abrupt. It would seem that two people of totally different cultures carved the interior and the coast petroglyphs.

What do we make of these carvings? Are they all in the same style, or are there shades of differences that we can detect? On first examination they all appear to be the same, more or less: very primitive, rather like the drawings of small children. Most of them are indeed crudely done, to our eyes, but we have to remember that they were carved by primitive man. Yet closer examination reveals that, within the primitive field of expression, there must have been traditionally accepted representations for many of the figures that were carved. Eyes, or round peck marks, sometimes enclosed within circles, are everywhere alike, though we do not know what they mean. Outlined and non-outlined faces at many sites are almost identical, and various spirit beings are executed in a similar technique and in similar representational forms. Thus we see a strong likeness between what is believed to be a "cannibal spirit" carved at Bella Coola and a similar figure at Yaculta Village, Quadra Island—several hundred miles apart. And again, square face masks (one imagines them to be) at Kulleet Bay, Ladysmith, on Vancouver Island are similar to square outlined faces at Port Neville in Johnstone Strait. Indeed, between the sites, the similarities are often striking.

It would seem that no carver went beyond accepted limits to express the figures of traditional spirits and beings, and in the mask faces there is scarcely any deviation. However, in figures that may be taken to represent the carver's personal guardian spirits, a total freedom seems to have been exercised. These so-called guardian spirit figures are fairly rare, and bear no similarity to each other, even at the same sites.

This is not to suggest that all the carvings on the coast were done in the same period. Several periods seem to be represented. At some sites, and often on one rock face, one detects differences in technique that suggest a wide range of time between the carvings. At Port Neville, for instance, at least three distinct periods are represented in the different techniques used to carve the glyphs on a single slab of bedrock. At Francesco Point on Quadra Island, though all the petroglyphs are much eroded and obviously of considerable age, two very different styles exhibit differences that can be attributed to a fairly wide spread of time.

levels. That is to say, these carvings are submerged at medium to high tides. Carvings so located are to be found from Bella Coola southward into Washington.

It is difficult to imagine an ancient petroglyph carver waiting for extreme low tide in order to begin his work, and to be constantly interrupted by the rising tides, while, close by, other rock surfaces well above the high tide reach offered good opportunities for carving. It is more reasonable to believe that the rock surfaces on which he worked were, at the time, situated well above high tide level. This could only mean that at the time these carvings were done, the sea level, in relation to the land level, was considerably lower than it is at present. In most places a difference in tide level of at least twelve feet would be required to allow the carvings to stand above the high tide mark. This leads us into a study of the surficial geology of the Pacific Coast, a subject on which little investigation has been done to date. However, so far as is known at present, it is probable that the sea level was, in most coastal places, some fifteen feet lower than at present, about eight thousand years ago.

One strongly hesitates to place the age of any of the petroglyphs that far back, however, and there is some reason to believe that world tidal fluctuations two, three and four thousand years ago resulted in somewhat lower tide levels on the Northwest Pacific Coast, from which time the tide may have risen regularly in infinitesimal degrees. Possibly some of the petroglyphs were carved during one of these fluctuations.

In many places the possibility must be considered that erosion of shorelines has undermined the carved boulders and lowered them to the beach at present tide levels. Shoreline erosion has always been a factor, and at places such as storm-beaten Cape Mudge, it continues at a rapid pace. Yet in instances where petroglyphs have been carved on bedrock at low tide level, one can only conclude that the petroglyphs were done at existing tide levels, or that tide levels were substantially lower when the carvings were done.

It must be pointed out, however, that at least a few of the coast petroglyphs are of recent origin. At Cape Alva, Washington, there is a carving of a sailing ship—proof positive that the petroglyph was done within the historic period, and leading to the question as to whether the rest of the carvings at that site are also of modern origin. Another carving at Bainbridge Island, Puget Sound, is believed to have been done, at least in part, within this century. At Fort Rupert, on Vancouver Island, one of the carved figures on the beach is said to have been carved in the mid-nineteenth century to mark the spot where a slave was killed and eaten during a cannibal society ceremonial. At Cape Mudge, Quadra Island, a few very crudely pecked figures on the

10   As well as differences in rock carving techniques, differences in the degree of erosion of carvings at the same site lead to the conclusion that they were done over a wide span of time. Some beaches, of course, particularly in storm areas, are more subject to erosion than others, but at the same site one finds carvings so eroded as to be hardly distinguishable, while others bear a freshness as if they had been carved only a few hundred years ago. In the Bella Bella and Bella Coola areas the style and technique of the carvings are all of a kind, yet the degree of erosion of the granite beach boulders makes it clear that they were done over a long period of time. These are sites for the most part protected from storms.

Yet at Cape Mudge on Quadra Island, which is exposed to the full fury of the winter storms of the Strait of Georgia, the erosion of the petroglyphs is serious. These petroglyphs have been exposed to the wild sea for a very long time. Yet even here we see varying degrees of erosion on the carved granite beach boulders. Some of the figures are so faint that they can be seen in only special lights; others are clear enough, though severely weathered, and still others are so clear that they might have been carved a few hundred years ago—and, indeed, for all we know, might well have been carved in fairly recent times. If we bear in mind that most carvings were done on hard granite beach boulders, the factors of varying erosion play an important part in any attempt to ascribe age to the petroglyphs.

That many petroglyphs are extremely ancient is indicated by the fact that the majority are located on beaches at half to low tide levels. Others, as at Port Neville, Fort Rupert, and Return Passage at Bella Bella, are located on bedrock at the same tide beach rocks may have been the work of fairly recent carvers who attempted to emulate the style of the earlier petroglyphs. On the other hand, the site may have been used continuously as a shaman-shrine up to the historic period.

We can be certain that, for the most part, the petroglyphs were not the work of idle hands or "doodlers"—persons who recorded their childlike impressions upon beach boulders to while away the hours—though that has sometimes been offered as an explanation. Such an explanation does not take into account that many of the carvings are involved and highly stylized representations requiring considerable skill in technique. Nor does it take into consideration the fact that there are very real art values inherent in some of the carvings.

Many of the petroglyphs were most probably manifestations of the primitive religion of shamanism, and were likely carved by shamans at magico-religious centres or shrines. With few exceptions, the petroglyphs are far removed from sites of ancient villages, and it is unlikely that the common people of the time ever knew of their existence. Indeed, there may have been dire penalties for anyone of the uninitiated caught visiting the sites. This may be why knowledge of the petroglyphs has not come down to us, in the memory or mythology of the coast native. No Indian seems to know anything about them, and even when he knows of their existence, he shows less interest in them than the white man does. The Lekwiltok people of Cape Mudge, who have petroglyphs almost in front of their village, and whose children sometimes play upon the carved rock, say that the carvings were done long ago by the Spirit People. And who were the Spirit People? They shrug; that is what they have heard, but they do not know.

There can be little doubt that in most cases the petroglyphs along the coast represent old shaman cult-sites or shrines. A height of land, such as a cliff top, or a high shoreline bank, is often found at, or adjacent to the sites, as at Sproat Lake, Nanaimo Petroglyph Park, Cape Mudge and Francesco Point, and at places in the Bella Coola country.

These heights usually command great vistas of the sea and the surrounding countryside, of sunrises and sunsets. They are almost always far removed from known dwelling places. Other carvings are to be found in very isolated locations in inlets and bays. Still others are found inland from the shoreline in lonely, silent places that only the initiated could have found.

At certain sites, at Nanaimo, Cape Mudge and Meadow Island at Bella Bella, and in Washington, ceremonial bowls and rounded cups carved in the solid rock, are to be found with the petroglyphs, an indication that they were magico-religious shrines, and that the bowls were used for small offerings or sacrifices. Quite possibly at other sites, portable wooden or stone bowls were utilized. In this there may be some connection with the small sculptured bowls known to have been used by shamans and ritualists, found in the Gulf Islands and lower Fraser River country, and dated at approximately two thousand years. Indeed, it might be considered if the petroglyph carvings predated and were the forerunner of the small sculptured stone work of the Pacific Coast.

Further indication of cult sites comes from the fact that often one certain boulder, or a particular area of bedrock, was carved upon successively (as indicated by erosion) over ages of time: that certain rocks obviously had a magic or "power" and were used for carving over and over again until the whole available surface was utilized. Only then, it would seem, was an effort made to find another stone of comparable "power" on which to carve. Yet at these sites, many nearby rocks offering good smooth carving surfaces were completely neglected. The successive carvings on these rocks seem to establish a continuity that makes of the site a cult shrine extending over a long period.

Village on Quadra Island were probably carved for winter ceremonial activities. On the other hand, many spirit figures, the mask faces and the round peck marks, were likely of some symbolic or religious meaning.

In any event, the technique of carving was simple: a hard hammer stone used for pecking. This provided a rough outline of the figure. Subsequent fine pecking gave the outline evenness and uniformity.

A great amount of time would be required for most of the figures, even if they were done in simple pecked outline, such as one sometimes encounters. But most of the carvings show that a great deal of care was taken to achieve a deep incised line, to smooth the crudely pecked figure. And great care must have been taken to be sure that the rock did not shatter and ruin the line of a figure. Then, of course, time, vast time, eventually gave it the faint and softly eroded outline worked by ages of waves and weather.

But still, there must have been more to carving a petroglyph than that. The early shaman, fasting and communing with the spirits, perhaps upon a lonely cliff-top, or in a twilight glade, was able to conjure up the vision of one of the spirits or one of the supernatural or mythological beings that inhabited the spirit world. He was in the hands of the spirits; they transmitted their will and their power through him. If they were angry and threatening, he sought to appease them and do their bidding. If they were benevolent and helpful, he gained strength and magic from them.

Yet by no means all the spirits demanded that their images be carved on stone. One suspects that often whole centuries went by between the occurrence of one carving and another at the same site. Perhaps it was only those gods and spirits who were greatly feared or greatly adored that won their immortality in stone. That would be in keeping with primitive man's magico-religious manifestations throughout the world.

In any event, there came the time when it was required to carve an image upon stone, for whatever reason. Immediately, the problem became a purely artistic one—the rendering of an image into form. The image upon the mind had to be clear enough to be held for a considerable period of time, while a boulder or bedrock surface was selected that held special power. In this search, many boulders offering good carving surfaces were passed by, and it would seem, only a certain stone was chosen. Then began the work of carving, chipping away with a stone hammer for days, perhaps for weeks, while all the time the vision of the spirit image that was taking form had to be held clearly in the carver's mind, until at last it was done, a thing of wonder then, a thing of wonder now after all the centuries.

12   It is assumed that these shrines were occupied only intermittently, when the shamans left their primitive world behind and went into retreat, to fast and dwell alone, to undergo ordeals, to commune with their guardian spirits, and conjure up visions of the supernatural beings and mythological creatures that occupied the shadows of their world. To primitive man, these spirits and beings had to be placated. They were everywhere about, sometimes benevolent, sometimes dangerous. And what better way to appease the spirits, and at the same time pay them tribute, than to carve their representations in stone for all time. So one might believe.

Some of the rock carvings, however, may have been created purely for ceremonial use. The Canadian archaeologist Harlan I. Smith has suggested that some of the petroglyphs near Bella Coola represent the faces of anthropomorphic beings, carved and used in connection with winter secret society ceremonials, where members would pound on the stones while singing. The cannibal figure of Bella Coola and a similar figure at Yaculta

Though their lines are often not straight, or perfectly rounded, though balance is sometimes lacking, it is evident that great care and devotion went into the carvings. And, here and there amid the sites, one sees evidence of the true artist at work, the desire to excel, to make a figure perfect, as the vision itself must have been perfect in the mind of the carver. The examples are not many, but those that are found are quite perfect works of art, as fine as primitive man has done anywhere in the world. There is the figure of the highly stylized bear at Englishman River on Vancouver Island, a figure imaginatively conceived, boldly executed, the eye of the bear strangely carved in a way that may have been the origin of the "eye" motif found in latter-day Northwest Coast art forms. At Kulleet Bay, Ladysmith, there is a figure of the rain god, a carving of rare perfection, a thing so marvellous that, coming upon it suddenly on the boulder strewn beach, leaves one spellbound. The eroded faint outline of the sea wolf at Francesco Point on Quadra Island, is another little work of art, a time darkened figure of a mythological sea creature that has a strange animation, and a form reminiscent of the latter-day art in which this same figure, more highly stylized, is often depicted. And then, among the art forms, there is the perfect, exquisitely wrought stylized deer's head at Port Neville in Johnstone Strait.

These are some of the works of true artists among the shaman carvers, and they convey to us the wonders that might have been created in very early times had there ever been a school of stone carving on the coast. But that was never to be: the artists were isolated in time and geography. They did their work, and probably no one else ever saw it until modern man cast his appreciative eye upon it. Out of the centuries of dark time, the wonder of these few artists is there for us to behold, crowded in with the more ordinary and primitive expressions of early man.

Thor Heyerdahl and other archaeologists, and very recently, the Russian A. P. Okladnikov* have noted that there exists a similarity between petroglyph carvings of the Northwest Coast and those of Far Eastern Siberia, particularly the Amur River region, and again, with certain carvings in the South Pacific Islands. So far as is known, these similarities lie mainly in the mask-like faces common to all three areas, though it must be noted that in the Amur River and the South Pacific masks, a spiraled ornamentation is dominant, whereas this is usually absent in the Northwest Coast. The similarities in areas are not particularly strange, however, for it is known that anciently the tribes of all three regions used masks in religious initiation rites into secret male societies. As has already been mentioned, the Canadian archaeologist Harlan I. Smith made note of such rites in connection with petroglyphs at Bella Coola.

Further studies of the petroglyphs of the three areas may reveal still other affinities. In the Amur River region, for instance, there are said to be carved and painted mythological monsters, fantastic creatures and grotesque versions of the human face, all apparently of very great antiquity. On the Canadian Coast, at Nanaimo, Sproat Lake, at Bella Coola and on Wrangell Island, Alaska, monsters and fantastic sea creatures are numerous. On Denman Island, at Cape Mudge and at Bella Coola there are several grotesque representations of the human face. It has further been noted that the Amur River basin contains drawings "of a human face with rays going from it in all directions." At Cape Mudge there are two such representations of a sunburst enclosing a human face, both very ancient, very eroded.

13

*"The Petroglyphs of Siberia", Scientific American Magazine, August, 1969.

Northern Alaska

Distribution of the petroglyphs on the coast varies greatly from region to region, from one Indian territory to another. On the whole, they appear to increase in numbers as one travels southward, though there are vast stretches of the coast on which no petroglyphs have been reported. Doubtless there will be more discoveries as the years go by, when population and travel increases, particularly in the north.

On the Brooks Range in Northern Alaska there is only one recognized site, some incised boulders in a *Kadigi,* or men's house, in a deserted village. Far to the south, on Kodiak Island, are two sites, one on a rock cliff and one on beach boulders. These petroglyphs depict human, non-outlined faces, whales, animals and pecked dots. The non-outlined faces are similar to those found in the Strait of Georgia area, particularly to a non-outlined face found at Cape Mudge on Quadra Island. As has already been noted, the mask-like face is typical of the whole range of coast petroglyphs. These Eskimo carvings are essentially no different from those found further south, so it may be assumed that the Eskimo shamanistic practices differed very little from those of the northern coast Indians.

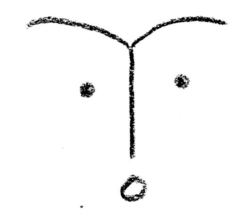

Left: Pecked mask designs, Kodiak Island, Alaska.
Right: Pecked mask at Cape Mudge, Quadra Island.

16

Redrawn from G. T. Emmons

At Sitka, in Tlingit Indian country, there is a carved boulder said to contain a complex representation of the creation myth, which is common to all the people of the coast. On Etolin Island there are several small beach boulders carved with a single figure on each. These are thought to belong to the Stikine Indians. Again, on Wrangell Island, near Fort Wrangell, there are more carved beach boulders containing fantastic sea monsters, among other representations.

Redrawn from G. T. Emmons

Pecked Mythological Creatures from Tlingit area, Southeastern Alaska.

Petroglyph at airport, 1 mile south of Wrangell, Alaska.

G. T. Emmons

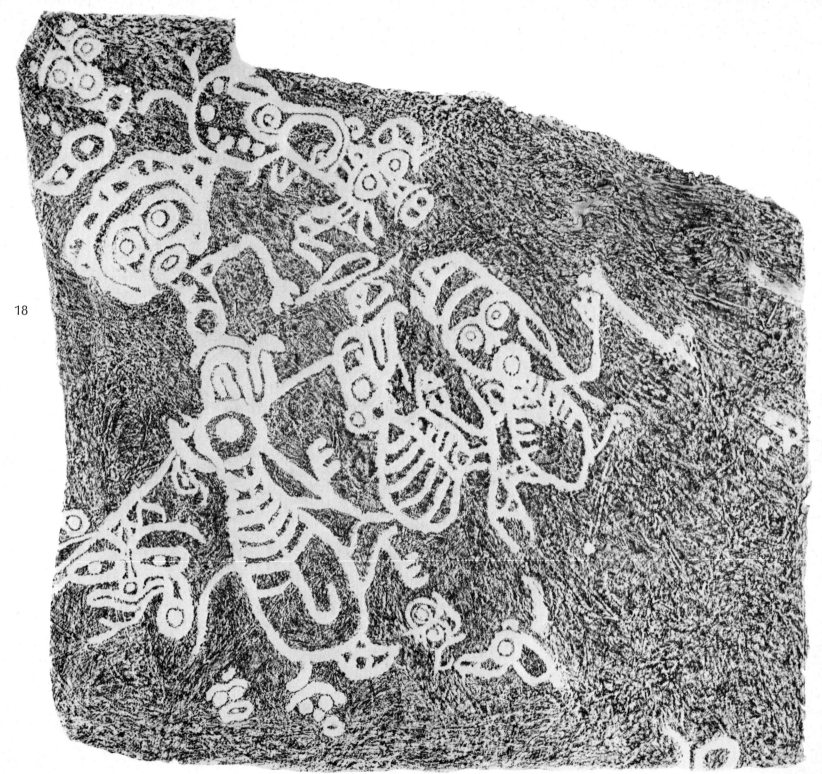

18

Terrace Photo Supply Ltd.

Tsimshian Territory

In the Tsimshian Indian territory, petroglyphs are reported at Metlakatla, in the Kitselas Canyon on the Skeena River, on Gold Creek (Kleanza Creek), on the Naas River near Canyon City, and again below Greenville (Lackalzap); at Pitt Island in Grenville Channel, and in Lowe Inlet. The only intaglio carving on the coast is found at Roberson Point, Prince Rupert. In Kitselas Canyon, there is a small carving of a blackfish or killer whale, which relates the river carvings to the coast type of petroglyphs.

Two petroglyphs are reported in Douglas Channel, in the Kitimat area, but they have not yet been investigated, and little is known of them. The Kitimat people were linguistically Kwakiutl, since they spoke the Haisla dialect of the Kwakiutl language. In their cultural relationships, however, they were Tsimshian. Kitimat is a Tsimshian name.

There is a group of carvings near the old village of the Hartley Bay Tsimshian, which are quite well known, and are said to have been associated with secret society initiates.

The most southerly of the Tsimshian petroglyphs is on the north side of Myers Pass, Princess Royal Island.

Rubbing of Ringbolt Island petroglyphs in the Kitselas Canyon, Skeena River, showing mask faces with headdresses, spirit beings and sea creatures. The rubbing was done by the Skeena Secondary School Archaeological Club.

Sea creatures carved in Kitselas Canyon, Skeena River.

D. Walker

20

An intaglio carving on Roberson Point, Prince Rupert.
Indian legend says that this is the impress of a man
who fell from heaven.

Carved stone, Mosquito design (approx. 30'' X 18'') at Kispiox.
Geologically, this stone is believed to belong to the
Bella Coola Valley area.

B.C. Provincial Museum

22

Next we come to the territory of the Northern Kwakiutl, where there are five known sites. The most northerly of these is on the east arm of Mussel Inlet, near Mathieson Channel. In the Bella Bella area itself are four sites. One site, on Denny Island, contains an outlined face mask and a non-outlined face consisting of only eyebrows and eyes.

Nearby, on Meadow Island, is the most interesting of the Northern Kwakiutl sites. It is the first northern site to depict the "copper," the wealth symbol of all the tribes of the Northwest coast. It is in a woodland glen on the island, above the beach, on a slab of bedrock. The whole rock outcropping is covered with carvings, many being representations of the "copper," others of grotesque human figures and mask faces. Most notable of all is an oblong ceremonial bowl carved in the solid rock, presumably for the purpose of holding small sacrifices or offerings. It is truly a shaman's site, remote, eerie and known only to the initiated. Even today, it cannot be found without a guide.

Another Northern Kwakiutl site is in Return Passage, on a slab of bedrock on a small wooded point of land. The figures, mask faces, fish and spirit creatures, are pecked on soft rock that is washed by the tide. These petroglyphs appear to have been done in the same period as the Bella Coola carvings.

Mask face, on the shoreline, Return Passage, Bella Bella.

Figure of a fish, Return Passage, Bella Bella.

24

Still another Northern Kwakiutl site consists of two panels about halfway up the north shore of Namu Lake. They are believed to have been carved in the early historic period. One panel depicts a canoe with four men in it, the other panel is of a canoe with a solitary man. A local legend goes with this site, to the effect that four men set off to the head of the lake to hunt bear, that a grizzly killed all but one of the party who made his escape back to the old village of Namu.

Fish and mask face at half tide, Return Passage, Bella Bella.

Spirit being, Return Passage, Bella Bella.

Bella Coola

26

National Museum of Canada

The Northern Kwakiutl in the Bella Bella country were separated from the Bella Coola Indians by a language barrier, rather than by any very clearly defined territorial lines. The Bella Bella speak the Heiltsuk language, a dialect of Kwakiutl, whereas the Bella Coola language is a member of the Salish language family. On the map, the Bella Coola area is shown as extending westward almost to Cascade Inlet on the north shore of Dean Channel, and including the eastern tip of King Island. The Bella Coolas were more oriented towards the heads of the inlets and the river systems in their territory, whereas the Bella Bella were a more truly coastal people. The two tribes seemed to have lived in comparative peace for a long period of time, and probably had fairly close cultural intercourse. There is historic evidence that the Bella Coola passed peacefully through the Bella Bella coastal territory when travelling to other parts of the coast.

One would, therefore, expect the Bella Coola petroglyphs to be somewhat like those of the Bella Bella Kwakiutl, and this is, in fact, the case. In the inlets and along the rivers we see carvings

Pecked head of a fish at Bella Coola.

Petroglyph site on top of a rise above the Bella Coola River.

28

National Museum of Canada

National Museum of Canada

of the same style and technique as at Bella Bella, and in fact, the same style extends southward as far as Washington.

There is no doubt that the Bella Coolas and the Bella Bellas were very fond of carving on rock. There are more petroglyph sites in their territory than in any similar sized area on the Pacific Coast, but the country is so inaccessible that few people ever see them. Representations of the "copper," the wealth symbol, appear at several sites. At Elcho Harbour there is a figure of a so-called cannibal spirit that is very similar to a figure at Cape Mudge. Mortars, or bowls carved in the rock, are found at three sites. As elsewhere on the coast, mask faces, outlined and non-outlined, are numerous.

Harlan I. Smith has said that some of these carvings were used in association with winter ceremonials of a secret society, possibly the cannibal society, and that the Indians drummed upon the carved rocks during the ceremony.

Carvings on a boulder just below high tide line, at the mouth of Elcho (Alice) Harbour, Dean Channel. The central figure with outstretched hands is said to be that of a cannibal spirit. The "copper", a wealth symbol, is in the lower right corner.

A wolf figure near Nootasum River, Bella Coola Valley.

National Museum of Canada

Figure of a cannibal spirit, Elcho Harbour, Bella Coola.

Pecked bird figure in the Bella Coola valley, opposite the mouth of Nootasum River.

32

33

National Museum of Canada

Petroglyphs in the canyon of the Bella Coola River.

Petroglyphs on the west side of the canyon, seventy feet deep,
about a mile south of the Bella Coola River
and Mackenzie Highway.

34

On the Queen Charlotte Islands, in Haida territory, there is only one petroglyph, located about a mile from Skidegate. The carving is shallow pecked, showing human heads and mask faces. In 1900, Dr. C. F. Newcombe* investigated the site, and the Indians at that time could offer no explanation of the carvings.

*At the turn of the century considered to be the foremost authority on Pacific Northwest Indians.

Southern Kwakiutl

At Fort Rupert, in Southern Kwakiutl territory, the local Indians 35
in 1920 told Harlan I. Smith, the Canadian archaeologist, that the
carvings there had been done "before animals were turned into
men." Dr. C. F. Newcombe, however, was told that several of the
carvings were quite recent. The petroglyphs are in two groups.
One group, three quarters of a mile west of the old fort site, consists of three faint mask faces, two carved on sandstone beach
boulders, and one on a granite boulder. Eastward, on the beach
in front of the site of the old fort, is a slab of bedrock sandstone
on which several petroglyphs are carved. One carving is believed
to represent the sea monster la'kin. The remainder of the carvings are of small faces and masks eroded in the sandstone, and
covered at medium tide. One of these faces is said to have been
carved on that spot on the beach where a slave of the Nanaimo
tribe was hacked to pieces and eaten during a cannibal society
ceremonial in the mid-nineteenth century.

All the carvings at Fort Rupert are washed by the tide, and
being carved on sandstone, are subject to rather rapid erosion.
It is doubtful if they are of great antiquity.

*This carved stone was found in the sea off the mouth of the
Cluxewe River, northern Vancouver Island.*

36

The only other rock carvings found in Southern Kwakiutl country are the Cluxewe Stone and a petroglyph near Kingcome Inlet. The Cluxewe Stone is a slab of sandstone brought up in a seine fishing net from five fathoms of water off the mouth of the Cluxewe River, northern Vancouver Island, in 1967. The carved head, in profile on this stone is a marvellous example of Kwakiutl carving at its best, and is the only example of stone sculpture of its kind. When brought to the surface, the stone was covered with barnacle growth. There is no explanation for how long it had been in the sea, or how it came to be there. It may possibly have been a portable ceremonial stone of some kind, lost from a canoe.

The petroglyph near Kingcome Inlet is on the low tide beach in Greenway Sound, opposite the mouth of Kingcome. It is a marvellously executed head of a human, carved from a rock bluff in relief—the only relief carving known on the Pacific Coast.

Carved sandstone boulder, west end of the beach at Fort Rupert, Vancouver Island.

Petroglyphs carved on bedrock, Fort Rupert, Vancouver Island.

Eroded carvings of mask faces on the beach at Fort Rupert.

Nootkan Territory

George Kinney

There are five known sites in Nootkan territory, on the west coast of Vancouver Island. At Nootka are two human figures of a male and female. The unique feature of these carvings is that the outline of the figures is achieved by double pecked lines, a technique found elsewhere only at one site, in Washington.

Another site is at Quisitis Point, between Wickanninish Bay and Florencia (Wreck) Bay, beside the marker of the 49th parallel. The carvings are very crude and eroded. One figure shows a huge fish eating a smaller fish, and nearby, pit markings similar to those found elsewhere on the coast.

Near Pachena Point, south of Barkley Sound, a shoreline sandstone cave contains two small carvings of the figure 8, and on a fallen slab of the cave wall, several fish figures.

At Clo-oose are well known carvings of sea birds, probably the puffin.

A fine group of carvings is located at the inland site of Sproat Lake. The Hopatcisath, an extinct tribe, once made their home on the shores of the lake, and might have been a Salishean-speaking people who became "Nootkanized" in both speech and culture. Certainly these carvings in no way resemble the other Nootkan petroglyphs. They are distinctly in the Nanaimo carvings style, and for this reason pictures of them are shown with the Nanaimo petroglyphs.

Male petroglyph figure at Nootka.

40

George Kinney

Nootka female figure pecked on granite.

Salish of the Strait of Georgia

The most northerly petroglyph in what was traditionally the territory of the Salish of the Strait of Georgia occurs at Grey Creek, seven miles up the east side of Loughborough Inlet. Here is found a large granite beach boulder at about high tide mark, containing two pecked dots, each surrounded by five or six concentric circles. They apparently form the eyes of a mask face, outlined. Another face, non-outlined, is on the same boulder. No other carvings are known in the neighborhood.

One of the most interesting petroglyph sites on the Pacific Coast is at Port Neville in Johnstone Strait. The carvings are located on the west side of the tip of Robber's Nob, on a large, flat-lying outcrop of bedrock granite that has been smoothed and grooved by glacial action. All the carvings are exposed at low tide, most are covered at half tide, and all are awash at high tide.

This site is very protected, and the carvings are subject only to the erosive action of the tides and small westerly squalls. Nevertheless, some of the carvings are quite faint and eroded, while others are fresh and clear in outline. It is quite evident that the carvings were done in at least three widely spaced periods, and three different styles of carving are represented in the group— styles varying both as to types of figures, and techniques of carving.

Stylized deer's head, Port Neville, Johnstone Strait.

42

What one may take to be the oldest style at Port Neville resembles the pecked figures found elsewhere from Bella Coola to Washington—the true west coast style—represented most clearly at Cape Mudge and Bella Coola. In this style, care was usually taken to achieve a good smooth incised line. A control and mastery of technique is evident. This appears to be the earliest, most primitive of styles, and is quite well represented at Port Neville. Also at Port Neville are square outlined human faces. Similar squared faces appear at Yellow Rock, on Denman Island, and at Kulleet Bay, Ladysmith.

Another style at Port Neville is much more primitive and less well executed than the former style, though probably not so old. This is represented in scratched and roughly chiselled figures, mostly human, and it seems clear that they were hastily done, with no effort made to smooth or finish the work. These figures resemble, to some extent, the crudely pecked figures at Harewood Plain, Nanaimo.

Pecked head at Port Neville, Johnstone Strait.

Fish with monster head, Port Neville.

44   The third style found at Port Neville is very distinctive, and is to be seen in two carvings that may be called the "northern style," for both these carvings exhibit a strong northern influence. One of the two figures represents a highly stylized deer's head, and is in itself as fine a work of art as primitive man has done anywhere on earth. In style it seems directly related to the sea wolf at Francesco Point, the stylized bear at Englishman River and the Sun God at Kulleet Bay. The remarkable features of this style consist of a perfectly uniform pecked line, both in width and depth, the pecking being done with a different instrument than that used in the other styles, or else a vast amount more time was devoted to perfecting the figures. An obvious mastery of technique and form has produced two of the most beautiful figures among all the glyphs of the coast. Three circles, two of them bisecting, appear to be the work of the same carver.

    The area of the petroglyphs contains substantial midden, and was an early habitation site. The midden appears to extend across the fine pebble beach to below medium tide level. Blue glass beads and chipped arrowheads were collected from this site and are in the Campbell River Museum. It is doubtful if the site was a village when the petroglyphs were carved. They would appear to be quite ancient.

Square and round faced spirit figures (chalked), Port Neville.

Forward Harbour

In Forward Harbour, Wellbore Channel, are three carved granite beach boulders, very near the head of the harbour, in front of a group of logging camp buildings.

Of the three boulders, the most easterly is a large flat-lying rock containing outlined and non-outlined faces, a human figure, possibly female, beside a frog, and a skeletal fish in "X-ray" view, with a curiously shaped head not unlike the fish head at Port Neville. The human figure on this rock is the largest glyph, central to the others.

A short distance west on the beach are two boulders containing very crudely pecked faces. They are, in fact, so crudely done that one suspects them of being the work of doodlers—Indians with idle time on their hands who tried to emulate the better carving on the flat-lying rock. All three boulders are washed by the medium tide.

Chalked figures on the beach, Forward Harbour, Wellbore Channel.

Yaculta Village

46

Two hundred yards north of the Yaculta Indian village near Cape Mudge on Quadra Island, in Discovery Passage, are two spirit figures pecked on a beach boulder washed by the tide. The figures take the shape of grotesque humans. One of them is very similar to a "cannibal" spirit figure at Bella Coola. The face of one of the figures is frowning and forbidding: the other has a happy, smiling face. No Indian of the area knows anything about them.

Spirit figure at Yuculta Village, Discovery Passage.

Grotesque spirit figure at Yuculta Village, Discovery Passage.

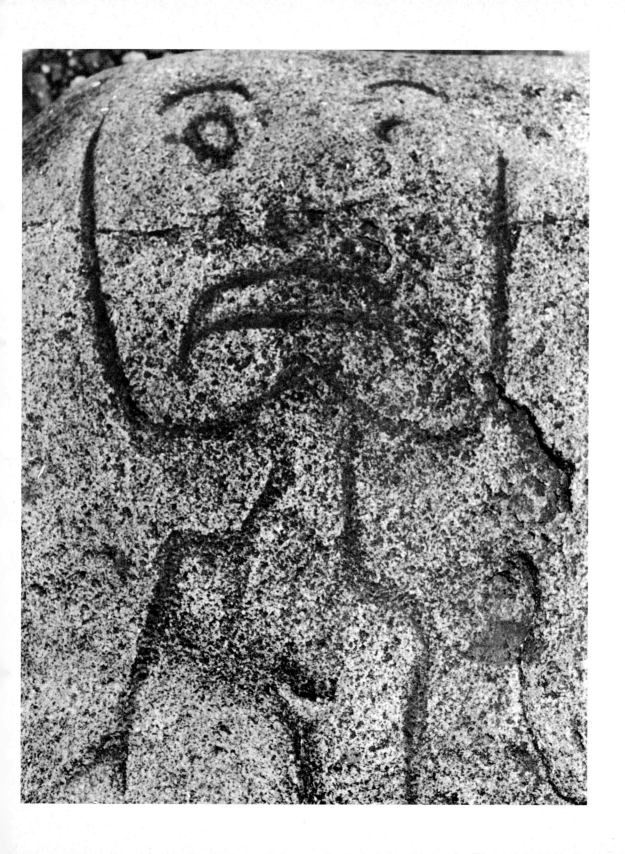

Cape Mudge

More carvings are to be found at Cape Mudge, Quadra Island than at any other site on the Pacific Coast. Altogether, there are twenty-six beach boulders carved in one fashion or another. All lie on the boulder-strewn beach and are covered by high tides. Some of the boulders are large and have strange figures carved on them. Others are small round boulders scattered on the beach, carved with sunbursts and faces. Several of the rocks contain only round peck markings, so common on the coast and in Washington. It is believed that these round peck marks are to be found on South American rivers, in Africa, and in Siberia. One boulder contains a carved bowl or receptacle, possibly used for offerings and small sacrifices.

The style of the figure carvings is the same as at Bella Coola, Forward Harbour and the Washington sites, but the sea serpent, zoomorphic and fish figures are completely absent here. There are two grotesque human representations, many mask faces, the heads of spirit beings, and one bird figure, the latter visible only at extreme low tide. The representation of faces is highly stylized, consisting most often of nothing but eyes and mouth, the eyes being pecked dots enclosed in a single circle, the mouth usually oval. Nose and ears are generally omitted. When the body and limbs are shown in figures, the hands are always three or four fingered.

A spirit face pecked on granite, Cape Mudge.

Mask faces and round pit markings on boulder washed by the tide at Cape Mudge.

50

It is probable that Cape Mudge was an important early shaman site, associated with the high cliff nearby. There are midden remains on the Cape, but as we know from Captain Vancouver's Journal, it was occupied as a village site at the beginning of the historic period, and no doubt was a defensive location in the summer raiding season. There is no evidence whatever to indicate that it was a habitation site in very early times.

Eroded spirit being at Cape Mudge.

Sunburst face, Cape Mudge.

*Bird figures (chalked) at low tide, Cape Mudge,
(note barnacle growth).*

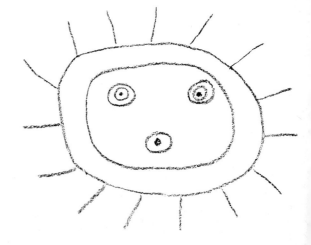

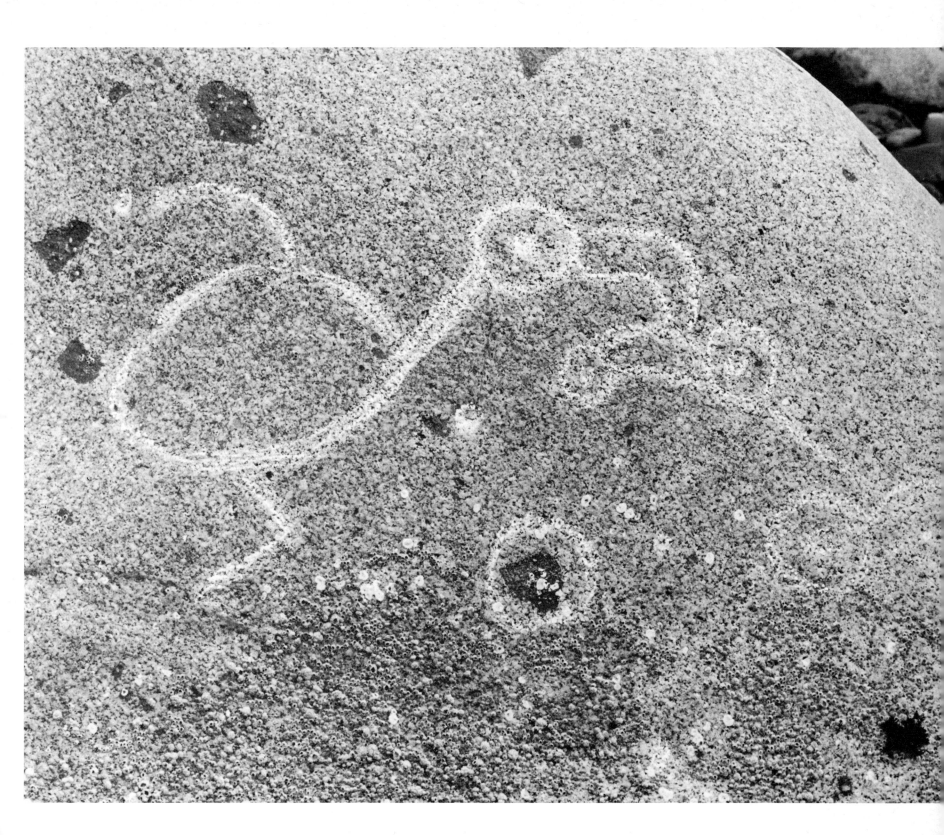

Carved beach boulder, Cape Mudge.

Ceremonial bowl carved into a beach boulder, Cape Mudge.

54

Non outlined mask face at Cape Mudge, similar to a figure in Alaska.

Figures and round pit marks on a beach boulder at Cape Mudge.

56

On Francesco Point, Quadra Island, on the beach in front of some abandoned fishermen's shacks, which was once the site of an Indian summer village, are four petroglyph beach boulders of granite. One boulder contains three outlined faces which may represent masks. Very close to this is another boulder with a single non-outlined face. Another nearby boulder further west on the beach shows carvings so eroded as to be now unidentifiable.

All these carvings on the outer point show very considerable erosion, perhaps more so than the carvings at nearby Cape Mudge. Here the winter storm action is more violent, and the petroglyphs are completely exposed. It is probable that several carved boulders have been overturned on this beach through the ages.

At Dogfish Bay, half a mile north of Francesco Point, are two carved boulders. One is a small basalt boulder with a single human face. It lies at low tide-mark and is very eroded. A few

Chalked mask faces on the beach at Francesco Point, Quadra Island.

feet away, close to the shoreline and near the high tide level, is a large boulder completely covered with carvings and round pit markings. We do not know the meaning of the round pit markings, but close examination shows that they were carefully done, finely executed by pecking, and then grinding and smoothing the inner surface. Each peck mark must have taken a considerable length of time to complete. Perhaps they represent the skeletal eye and nose sockets of spirit faces, perhaps the faces of the dead.

On the same boulder at Dogfish Bay, facing the sea, there is a remarkable carving of what might be called a sea serpent. It bears a startling resemblance to the mythological Kwakiutl sea wolf. It is pecked out in perfect outline, and is a little work of art. It is impossible to believe that the carver who did this figure pecked the cruder, simpler carvings on the same rock, though all appear to be of the same age.

The Sea Wolf at Francesco Point, pecked on granite.

58

The only petroglyph on Cortes Island, at the north end of the Strait of Georgia, is midway between Smelt Bay and Manson's Landing, just north of the old Indian village of Paukeanum. The glyph depicts the naturalistic outline of a fish or possibly a whale. The carving measures nine feet across, and is pecked on a huge granite boulder on the beach. It is visible only at low tide.

The carving suffers somewhat from vandalism. Part of the outline has been filled with a cement grout and a settler has carved his name on the rock.

Cortes Island fish, nine feet in length.

Petroglyphs of birds, Yellow Rock (chalked), Denman Island.

On the eastern mainland side of the Strait of Georgia a huge 59 stretch of coastline from Desolation Sound to the Fraser River is completely devoid of petroglyphs. On the Vancouver Island shore, the petroglyphs continue southward from Cape Mudge in Discovery Passage.

A fine group of carvings is to be found at Yellow Rock, on the south end of Denman Island, adjacent to the lighthouse, on bedrock granite. A very large surface is covered with rock pictures, and more were destroyed in blasting for the erection of the lighthouse. The site has a larger variety of figure representations than any other on the coast—whales and fish, sun and stars, animals, birds and grotesque supernatural creatures bearing some resemblance to human beings. Also noteworthy is the presence of

60

innumerable mask faces set in square outlines, similar to those at Port Neville and Kulleet Bay. It would seem that the total surface carved consists of two separate areas, the figures in each differing widely in style, as though done by two carvers, or in two widely spaced periods.

On nearby Hornby Island there are four petroglyph sites, and possibly more unreported. These show human forms, deer, and finback whales, and are carved by pecking and rubbing in the soft sandstone. All are subject to rather rapid erosion. It is not likely that they are very old.

Human form pecked on sandstone at Whaling Station Bay, Hornby Island.

Carving of a deer, north shore of Hornby Island.

Human form pecked on sandstone in a creek bed at Hornby Island.

62

63

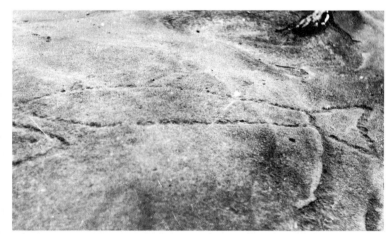

National Museum of Canada

National Museum of Canada

Yellow Rock carvings (chalked), south end of Denman Island.

Petroglyph of a whale on sandstone between tides, north side of Hornby Island.

Anthropoid figure at the head of Whaling Station Bay, Hornby Island. Note that the foot has a high heel.

64

Suns, fish and supernatural creatures carved on Yellow Rock, south end of Denman Island. (chalked)

Parksville

An interesting petroglyph site is located three miles south of Parksville, on the gorge of the Englishman River, Vancouver Island. The carvings are at the top edge of the gorge on exposed bedrock.

The petroglyphs consist of three figures, one very large, of a highly stylized bear, and two smaller ones, probably bear heads. Two other carvings, one a human head, and one possibly a crawfish, are destroyed by recent cleavage of the rock. Vandals have carved and painted names near the figures.

The stylized bear figure is remarkable as a pure work of art, and because it is done in profile and expresses in its flowing lines and space filling technique, much that is contained in the latter-day art forms of the Kwakiutl and other northern Indians. The eye of this bear is also reminiscent of the "eye" motif used in northern carving.

The Englishman River petroglyphs are of considerable age, as is evident in the degree of erosion by time and weather. The fact that the bear figure is done in profile makes it the one remarkable exception to the petroglyph style of full-faced, outlined and non-outlined figures so common on the coast.

Stylized bear at Englishman River, pecked on sandstone.

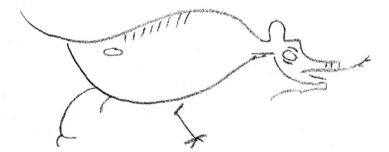

66

There are several petroglyph sites in the Nanaimo area, the best known being at Petroglyph Park on the Island Highway, two miles south of the city. This site is located on a smooth outcropping atop a "hogback" ridge paralleling the harbour front to the east, near Chase River.

These petroglyphs, together with those at Sproat Lake, are altogether different from anything else on the coast, both in technique and figure representations. The technique used seems to have been pecking and abrading to obtain a clear, smooth incised line. In places where the figures have been long protected by moss and earth, the incised lines are from one and a half to two inches in depth, and an inch in depth where exposed.

All the figures are highly stylized; there is not a naturalistic representation among them. One slab of rock, nearly horizontal, is completely covered with figures of various monsters in outline, resembling birds, wolves, lizards, and supernatural marine creatures with numerous appendages along the back that are unknown in any living thing. One monster is shown as having swallowed a man.

Running dragon, Cedar-by-the-Sea, Nanaimo.

Fish and mythological monsters, Nanaimo Petroglyph Park.

68   The area is bisected by parallel incised straight lines, some forty feet in length. There are five of these lines. There is another half line that extends from the crest of the hill and runs sixteen feet down to intersect another incised line that crosses the face of the stone to form right angles with two of the five long channels. About five feet below this cross line, and at about the centre of the area, there is a carved circular bowl two and a half inches in depth and forty inches in diameter. The bowl undoubtedly had some ceremonial significance.

Without question, the site has been a large shamans' cult centre in early times. It would seem that not only the area of the carvings, but the whole of the hogback ridge was used for ceremonials.

A remarkable petroglyph site was discovered in 1969 above the Nanaimo River, five miles south of Nanaimo City. The carvings were discovered during land clearing for a homesite by Mr. & Mrs. Perry Monsell, the property owners. So far, thirty two glyphs have been exposed, consisting of human, semi-human, bird-like, animal, mythological and dragon-like figures. They are pecked into fairly horizontal bedrock sandstone near the top of low hills. Stylistically, they are very closely related to the glyphs at nearby Nanaimo Petroglyph Park, and to those at Sproat Lake. They are executed in a beautifully fluid style, full of motion and feeling. Most of the human and part human figures appear to be wearing headdresses, and some have phallic representations.

Petroglyph on Point extending south from Brechin mine, near Nanaimo, B.C.

A human glyph with head-dress carved on sandstone at Monsell Petroglyph Site, Cedar District, Nanaimo.

Stylized birds at Nanaimo Petroglyph Park.

The Monsell petroglyph site is undoubtedly one of the finest and most important known anywhere. The site is located on Wilkinson Road, beside the Nanaimo River, in the Cedar District.

Another interesting Nanaimo petroglyph is the Jack's Point rock, now moved to the grounds of the Nanaimo Museum. The Indian legend attached to this panel of carvings is to the effect that the fish figures were originally painted on the rock by a shaman-priest whose daughter was changed into a dog salmon. Probably the painted rock was later carved by the same priest, by pecking and abrading to form beautiful stylized representations of the flounder, the spring salmon with long hooked nose, the hump back salmon, the cohoe and the dog salmon. The head and beak of a pelican has been carved as a space filler. Succeeding shamans made food offerings to a fire built at the foot of the carved rock. These fish carvings are definitely in the same style as the carvings at Petroglyph Park.

Figure of a deer pecked on sandstone, Nanaimo Petroglyph Park.

Priest's rock, Jack's Point, now removed to the Nanaimo Museum.

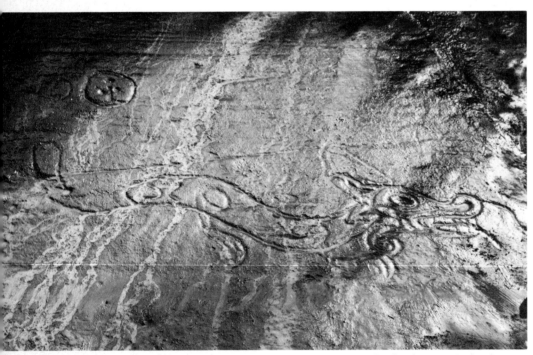

*A dragon-like figure at the Monsell petroglyph site, Cedar
District, Nanaimo. This figure is similar to dragon glyphs at the
Nanaimo Petroglyph Park and at Sproat Lake.*

Hermaphrodite figure at Harewood Plain, Nanaimo.

One of the strangest carvings on the Pacific Coast is to be 73 found on the so-called Harewood Plain of Nanaimo, a five acre area of flat-lying bedrock covered with a thick growth of moss. This is an inland site, far removed from the shoreline. Here are two sets of carvings, one a very faint, crudely chipped outline of a snake and a dancing man. The other carving, somewhat removed from the first, is of a human figure possessing hair on the right side of the head, a right female breast, and a phallus. It is probably a hermaphrodite figure, and the only one encountered on the coast. It is doubtful if the area of Harewood Plain was ever a shamans' site, and one can only surmise that the carving was done by someone of a hermaphrodite nature permanently exiled from the tribe. The carving is crude and not at all in the well known style of the Nanaimo petroglyphs.

On Gabriola Island, near Nanaimo, there is said to be a petroglyph rock, close to Digman's wharf at the south end of the island. Another petroglyph is reported at Helen's Point, Mayne Island, in Active Pass.

Mythological monster at Nanaimo Petroglyph Park.

Carved sea serpents at Nanaimo Petroglyph Park, similar to serpents on the Monsell site on the Nanaimo River, and at Sproat Lake.

74

Located in the Provincial Park at Sproat Lake, a group of well known petroglyphs are so similar to the Nanaimo Petroglyph Park carvings, in technique and figure representations, that they belong to the same "school."

Philip Drucker, in his book "Northern and Central Nootkan Tribes," states that a Nootkan group called the Hopatchisat had made their home on the shores of Sproat Lake since time immemorial, and he notes that since they were actually east of the divide of the island and had fairly easy access to the east coast, they must have had considerable contact with the Salish of the Strait of Georgia. Edward Sapir, in his Nootkan studies, once suggested that the Hopatchisat might have been a Salish-speaking people who became "Nootkanised" in both speech and culture.

Mythological creatures carved on a rock face, Sproat Lake, Vancouver Island.

A serpent-like figure appears on the panel of petroglyphs here, and is also found at Nanaimo. This figure bears a close resemblance to that of a monster snake which had a deep root in the mythology of most of the Pacific Coast tribes. It was called the Haietlik by some and Hahektoak by others. According to C. F. Newcombe, the Indians believed that when the Thunderbird saw and wished to kill a whale, he hurled the Haietlik at it, which speared the whale like a harpoon. At times the Haietlik was said to take the form of a huge sea snake, at other times it became a sea monster. It had many wonderful attributes. Indians believed that to own even a small piece of the Haietlik was the highest possible magic obtainable. It meant wealth, power and success beyond all dreams.

The Serpent figure at Sproat Lake, Vancouver Island.

Carvings at Sproat Lake.

76

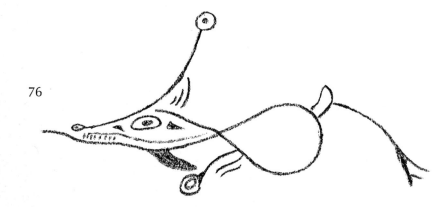

Two petroglyph sites are to be found in Kulleet Bay, Ladysmith. One site is on the north side of the bay, about midway between Deer Point and the head of the bay, and about thirty yards into the bush from the high water mark on the beach. The carvings are on a dried up creek bed, on a sandstone shelf, an eroded fracture of which catches a trickle of water to form a tiny woodland pool, five feet wide, fifteen feet long. The carvings are on the two inclined faces of the pool. W. A. Newcombe* was the first to record this site in 1931. It bears an Historic Objects Marker in good condition.

Today it is extremely difficult to find the location of this site in the bush, without the guidance of the local Indians. In prehistoric times it must have been a very remote place, and accessible only to the initiated. It seems clear that it was an inland shamans' site, used over a considerable period of time. Every available part of the sandstone ledge has been carved upon, and indeed, some figures have been partly carved over others, and even spaces originally left between the figures have been filled.

On the south side panel of the pool there are seventeen crowded figures over a length of ten feet. Two of the figures are human heads with hair or sunbursts, with square outlines. Another figure has a squared body similar to carvings at Yellow Rock and Port Neville. There is also a frog-man, a shrimp, birds, small fish and two remarkable figures that resemble the Salish mythical supernatural being Xai-Xai. Other figures cannot be discovered in the forest gloom.

Rain god at Kulleet Bay, Ladysmith, Vancouver Island.

Petroglyphs beside the magic pool, Kulleet Bay, Ladysmith.

*Son of Dr. C. F. Newcombe. One-time curator of the British Columbia Provincial Museum.

78

On the north side panel there are four figures, all human in aspect, not as well carved as those on the south side. One of these figures, of a monstrous head with four fingered hands, resembles a figure at Cape Mudge. The technique of carving all the figures would appear to be by pecking on the sandstone with no effort to smooth outlines by abrading. The site appears to be very old.

The other site in Kulleet Bay is on the south shoreline, about two miles south of the head of the bay. This petroglyph consists of a single sandstone boulder bearing one figure, said to be the rain god of the Kulleet Bay Indians, which has apparently entered into and become part of their mythology. It is a carving of rare artistry. Originally it was completely submerged in the bay, but loggers, whose booms continually snagged the rock, had it bulldozed from its extreme low tide position to its present location on the beach. At the time it was bulldozed it was not known to be a carving; that discovery was made afterwards.

The rain god of Kulleet Bay ranks with a few other carvings on the coast as a pure work of art, unrivalled by primitive man anywhere.

Frog-man at Kulleet Bay, Ladysmith.

Carvings at Kulleet Bay, Ladysmith.
The lower figure has a sunburst head-dress.

80

National Museum of Canada

On Salt Spring Island there is a fine beach boulder petroglyph of a face, the eyes formed by concentric circles. It belongs to the style of Cape Mudge and Bella Coola carvings, and is also similar to some glyphs in Washington. It is close to Fulford Harbour, near Centennial Park, on the road leading to Isabella Point.

On the southern tip of Vancouver Island, at Alldridge Point, at the west entrance to Beecher Bay, East Sooke, there is a petroglyph of a seal or sea lion that has escaped the hand of the vandal mainly for the reason that access to it is through private property.

The only reported petroglyph to be found on the lower Fraser River area is to be found at Doctor's Point on the west shore of Harrison Lake. It is called *kaiyama,* or the "little doctor." At last report the body and face of the figure were painted in red ochre. It is said that this petroglyph is similar in shape to the power or spirit boards used in the soul recovery ceremony of the Central Puget Sound Indians.

Petroglyph on Aldridge Point, Beecher Bay, East Sooke, Vancouver Island.

Puget Sound
and the Columbia River

J. Malcolm Loring

Essentially the same style of petroglyphs as are to be found on the Northwest Coast continues into Puget Sound and the lower Columbia River. In this area the use of concentric circles is very prevalent, as are the simple round pit markings. Mask faces are not often found, but where they occur they are highly stylized. A mortar, or carved ceremonial bowl, is located at Fisher's Landing, east of Vancouver, Washington. At Skamania, Washington, there is a huge boulder with a carved figure that is possibly a water serpent, not unlike carvings at Nanaimo and Sproat Lake, on Vancouver Island. Where human figures occur they have round heads and spread arms, and are pecked in simple outline. One of the petroglyphs at Cape Alava, Olympic National Park, depicts a sailing ship under full sail, proof positive that this, and possibly all the carvings at this site were done in the historic period.

At about the Dalles on the Columbia, the coast style of the petroglyphs seems to change radically to what might be called the interior style, and this latter style is to be found in the Willamette Valley and through Southern Oregon. It bears little likeness to the style prevalent on the Northwest Coast.

Pecked figure (chalked) at Cape Alava, Clallam County, Olympia National Park, Washington.

83

J. Malcolm Loring

*Petroglyph figures said to represent weeping whales and masks,
1½ miles south of Cape Alava, Clallam County, Olympic
National Park, Washington.*

Spirit figure (chalked), near Cape Alava, Washington.

84

J. Malcolm Loring

J. Malcolm Loring

J. Malcolm Loring

*North Bonneville Boulder, original site one mile S.W.
of North Bonneville, on the Columbia River.*

*Round pit markings, Fisher's Landing on the Columbia River,
9 miles east of Vancouver, Washington.*

*Guardian spirit figure (chalked) 1½ miles south of Cape
Alava, Olympic National Park.*

J. Malcolm Loring

J. Malcolm Loring

*Fish or whale, 52 inches in length, at the "Wedding Rocks",
1½ miles south of Cape Alava, Washington.*

*Carved ceremonial bowl at Fisher's Landing on the
Columbia River.*

88

J. Malcolm Loring

Victor Boulder petroglyph, on state highway 14A, between Vaughn and Allyn, Mason County, Washington.

Petroglyphs lightly pecked on basalt column near tidewater on the Columbia River. (Figures outlined in chalk). Cape Horn, Skamania County, Washington. The double outlined human figure is similar to one at Nootka, Vancouver Island.

90

Indian rock carving of a sailing ship, at the Wedding Rocks, Cape Alava, Washington.

Skamania Landing Boulder, on the Columbia River, Skamania, Washington. The figure may represent a water serpent.

J. Malcolm Loring

91

J. Malcolm Loring

Round pit markings and concentric circles at Gentry's Landing, on the Columbia River, 10 miles east of Vancouver, Washington.

Petroglyph boulder at Gentry's Landing on the Columbia River, Washington.

Bibliography

92 Boas, Franz 1891
"Felzenzeichnung Von Vancouver Island." Verhandlungen
der Berliner Gesellschaft fur Anthropologie, Ethnologie und
Urgeschichte, Ausserordenteliche Sitzunge am. 14.
February 1891: 160, fig. 162.

Barrow, Frances J. 1942
"Petroglyphs and Pictographs on the British Columbia Coast."
Canadian Geographical Journal, Vol. 24, pp. 94-101, Montreal.

Barrow, Francis J. No date
"Petroglyphs," Notebook 1, Manuscript in Provincial Museum,
Victoria, B.C.

Butler, B. Robert 1962
"Contributions to the Prehistory of the Columbia Plateau."
Occasional Papers of the Idaho State College Museum,
No. 9, Pocatello.

Cain, H. Thomas 1950
"Petroglyphs of Central Washington." University of Washington
Press, Seattle.

Codere, Helen
*"The Sxaixwe Myth of the Middle Fraser River, the Integration
of Two Northwest Coast Cultural Ideas."* Journal of American
Folklore, Vol. 61, No. 239, pp. 1-18.

Drucker, Philip 1943
"Archaeological Survey of The Northern Northwest Coast."
Bulletin of the Bureau of American Ethnology, Smithsonian
Institution, Washington, No. 133, Anthropological Paper,
No. 20, pp. 17-142.

Duff, Wilson 1961
"Preserving British Columbia's Prehistory." British Columbia,
Department of the Provincial Secretary. The Archaeological
Sites Advisory Board. Victoria.

Duff, Wilson 1956
*"Prehistoric Stone Sculpture of the Fraser River and
Gulf of Georgia."* Anthropology in British Columbia, No. 5.
Victoria, B.C.

Emmons, G. T. 1908
"Petroglyphs in Southeastern Alaska." American
Anthropologist, No. X.

Fyles, J. G. 1963
*"Surficial Geology of Horne Lake and Parksville Map Areas,
Vancouver Island."* Geological Survey of Canada.

Foster, Mrs. W. Garland 1926
"Stone Images and Implements and some Petroglyphs."
Vancouver Art, Historical and Scientific Association Museum
and Art Notes. Vol. 1, No. 3, pp 14-16.

Gjessing, Gutorm 1952
"Petroglyphs and Pictographs in British Columbia," in Sol Tax (ed.), Indian Tribes of Aboriginal America. International Congress of Americanists, Proceedings or Selected Papers, 29, Vol. 3, pp. 66-79.

Gjessing, Gutorm 1958
"Petroglyphs and Pictographs in the Coast Salishan Area of Canada." In Miscellania Paul Rivet . . . Publicaciones del Instituto de Historia, Primera Serie, No. 50, p. 270. Mexico City.

Grant, Campbell 1967
"Rock Art of the American Indians."
Thomas Y. Crowell Company, New York.

Hedden, Mark 1956
"The Mountain Sheep of Petroglyph Island." M. S. on file in the Washington State Museum, University of Washington, Seattle.

Heyerdahl, Thor 1953
"American Indians in the Pacific."
Rand McNally Company, New York.

Hole, Frank and Robert F. Heizer 1965
"An Introduction to Prehistoric Archaeology." Holt, Rinehart and Winston, New York and Toronto.

Keithahn, E. L. 1940
"The Petroglyphs of Southeastern Alaska." American Antiquity, Salt Lake City, Vol. VI, pp. 123-132.

Keithahn, E. L. 1953
"The tools of the Petroglyph Mason." Proceedings of the Fourth Alaskan Science Conference.

Krause, Aurel 1956
"The Tlingit Indians." Seattle (Trans. E. Gunther)

Leechman, Douglas 1952
"The Nanaimo Petroglyphs." Canadian Geographical Journal, Vol. 44, pp. 266-267. Montreal.

Newcombe, C. F. 1907
"Petroglyphs in British Columbia." Victoria Daily Times, Sept. 7. Also reprint with additions and corrections— Margison Brothers Printers, Oct. 17, 1907, Victoria.

Nordquist, D. L. 1962
"An Approach to Stylistic Analysis of Petroglyphs."
Part 1. Washington Archaeologist, Seattle, Vol. 6, No. 5, pp. 5-9; Part II, Washington Archaeologist, Vol. 6, No. 6, pp. 6-12, Part III. Washington Archaeologist, Vol. 6, No. 8, 9, 10, pp. 2-11.

Osborne, D. 1954
"Pictographs and Petroglyphs: What, Who, When and Why." Northwest Mineral News. Vol. 1, No. 4, pp. 17-24. Portland, Oregon.

94 Smith, H. I. 1907
"*Archaeology of the Gulf of Georgia and Puget Sound.*"
Memoirs of the American Museum of Natural History,
Vol. 4, part 6, pp. 303-441.

Smith, H. I. 1923
"*An Album of Prehistoric Canadian Art.*" Canada
Department of Mines, Geological Survey—Victoria
Memorial Museum Bulletin, Ottawa, 37, Anthropological
Series, Vol. 8.

Smith, H. I. 1924
"*The Petroglyph at Aldridge Point, near Victoria, British
Columbia.*" American Anthropologist, Monasha. (new series)
Vol. 26, No. 4, pp. 531-533.

Smith, H. I. 1925
"*A Prehistoric Petroglyph on Noiek River, British Columbia.*"
Man. 25, pp. 136-138.

Smith, H. I. 1927
"*A list of Petroglyphs in British Columbia.*" American
Anthropologist XXIX, No. 4, pp. 605-610.

Smith, H. I. 1936
"*The Man Petroglyph near Prince Rupert or the Man Who Fell
from Heaven.*" In Essays in Anthropology presented to
Alfred Louis Kroeber, University of California Press, Berkeley,
pp. 309-312.

Smith, M. W. 1946
"*Petroglyph Complexes in the History of the Columbia-Fraser
Region.*" Southwestern Journal of Anthropology (Sante Fe), 11,
No. 3, pp. 306-322.

Strong, W. D. and W. E. Schenck 1925
"*Petroglyphs of the Columbia River.*" American
Anthropologist, Monasha. (New series) Vol. 27, pp. 76-90.

Strong, W. D., W. E. Schenck and J. H. Steward 1930
"*Archaeology of the Dalles-Deschutes Region.*" University
of California Publications in American Archaeology and
Ethnology. Vol. 29, No. 1, pp. 1-154. Berkeley, Cal.

Acknowledgements

Thanks are due to the following for many   95
favours and for assistance:

Mr. Donald Abbott of the B.C. Provincial Museum
Mr. and Mrs. William Ballantyne
Miss Catherine Capes
Mr. Willard Ireland of the B.C. Provincial Archives
Mrs. Baron Jeffries
Mr. William Law
Dr. Douglas Leechman
Mr. J. Malcolm Loring of Portland, Oregon
The National Museum of Canada
Mr. Hugh Nasmith
Mr. Stanley J. Palmer
Mrs. George Rose
Mr. Neville Shanks
Mr. Phil Thornberg
Mr. D. R. Walker
and to numerous other persons on the coast
who have assisted in this work.

Photographs and line drawings by the author
except where credited.

The publisher gratefully acknowledges
a Canada Council grant which
has been passed on to the public.

The Author

Dane Campbell.

Edward Meade was born in Winnipeg in 1912. In 1930 he moved to British Columbia, making his headquarters on Vancouver Island from where, through the years, he travelled to all parts of the Pacific Coast studying the Indian tribes.

In World War II Meade was a platoon commander in a tank transporter outfit. After service overseas he returned to Vancouver Island, settled in Campbell River and took a particular interest in the Southern Kwakiutl Indians of northern Vancouver Island and Johnstone Strait. He has been termed an expert in this particular field and ranks as a very competent amateur archaeologist.

In 1949 he founded the Campbell River Historical Museum and served for many years as its curator on a voluntary service basis. As curator he travelled widely up and down the coast, collecting artifacts and items of Indian art for the Museum. He also collected many priceless items of Indian culture for the University of British Columbia Museum of Anthropology. It was during these travels that his attention was first drawn to the petroglyphs, the ancient Indian rock carvings, reported here and there on the coast by Indians, by commercial fishermen and by loggers. Meade set to work making a comprehensive list of all

the petroglyph sites on the coast and in his travels, year by year, he added to it. He investigated every report that came to him and, whenever possible, he personally visited the sites, sketching and photographing the carvings. He travelled by chartered plane, by boat with commercial fishermen, with Indians and sometimes by car. His travels took him from the far northern coast of Alaska to the Puget Sound area. It was a study extending over ten years. INDIAN ROCK CARVINGS is the result of these studies.

Meade is the author of the successful Canadian war novel, REMEMBER ME, first published by Faber and Faber, London, in 1946, reprinted by the Reprint Society and now published in a paperback edition by McClelland and Stewart, Toronto. He has also written many articles on the Indians and ethnology of the Pacific Coast.

Today Edward Meade resides in Campbell River with his wife, Winifred. A son, Michael, and daughter, Shawna, are attending universities in Western Canada. The book is dedicated to Michael who accompanied his father on many of the trips to the petroglyph sites.